Married2TheMission

NEW YORK CITY

The Bride of America at the Final Trump

––––––––––

Shadaria A. Allison

ISBN: 9781070377179

References:

Thomas, Tracey. "**Reported rapes across NYC increase by 39%, NYPD finds**". 2018

Toure, Madin. "**New York City Poverty Rate Hits Lowest Level since Great Recession**. 2018

Honan, Katie. "**New York City Murders on the Rise in 2018, NYPD Data Shows,** Spike comes as overall crime rate continues to fall".2018

(Google Public Data 2018) All definitions

History of New York (Wikipedia 2018)

biblehub.com (all scripture references)

2018 – First Quarter

Kate Spade and Anthony Bourdain committed suicide.
There were 23 school shootings before summer.
A fifteen-year-old was stabbed to death in the Bronx
An 18-year-old was stabbed in California by a Racist

CHILDISH GAMBINO MADE THE SONG AND VIDEO
OF
THE
CENTURY- *Thank you!*

Point A: Immigrant children were separated from their families
in an instant.
Point B: Donald Trump made an executive decision to stop
point A.

Racial profiling remained the same: **fatal, bias, and tragic**.

I moved to New York City, the *Bride of America*.

**"This book is dedicated to New York City. A city in
shackles, with the power to unshackle the entire nation".**

-Shadaria

This book is dedicated to those in power with the resources to change our nation.

For Christian Soto. For Kaila and Garrett.

For every homeless person, single mom, and troubled teen in America.

For those living in the extreme conditions of New York City.

For the Dreamers.

For my mother Shandra Allison.

For my father Maverick Gaither

My great grandparents who were builders and farmers

NANA and PAPA

For my son Ca 'ren Franklin.

For Black WOMEN.

For LATINA WOMEN.

For ASIAN WOMEN

For ALL WOMAN

FOR THE BLACK MAN

FOR THE BLACK CHURCH

For my people.

For the Allison's, Gaither's, and Montague's

For every person who has lost their lives due to police brutality and unjust causes of both war and racism.

For rape victims, drug addicts, and those crippled by systemic poverty.

For Immigrants.

For Native Americans.

For both my ancestors.

For President Donald Trump, leader of the "Free World".

For Joseph "Garrett" Lovelady, my 14-year-old godson whose Life ended too soon.

For Marlen-Ochoa Lopez.

"Give me your tired, your poor,
your huddled masses yearning to breathe free,
the wretched refuse of your teeming shore.
Send these, the homeless, tempest-tossed, to me:
I lift my lamp beside the golden door."

— Emma Lazarus

**Quote more famously recognized on the Statue of Liberty.*

Married2TheMission
NEW YORK CITY

The Bride of America at the Final Trump

―――――――

Shadaria A. Allison

Table of Contents

Introduction.

I took a job in the "Big Apple" during the summer of 2018.

New York City had been a distant *lover* of mine for quite some time. *After all, it was home.*

Living in the southern city of Birmingham, Alabama taught me a lot about life. It taught me that you shouldn't have a plethora of beautiful cathedrals built on elaborate street corners ornamented with sleeping homeless men on its stairs. It also taught me that if you are a police officer, it is considered bad manners to do a bag search at Harold Square train station (one of the busiest in Manhattan) on innocent youth, *especially when the **fifty less racially diverse humans in front of him, carried the same bag but not the same treatment.*** Birmingham also taught me that affordable housing shouldn't be controlled by selections called "lotteries". More importantly, affordable housing in NYC is NOT affordable *at all.* Do we really need a broker's fee, huge deposits, audacious credit scores, and both first and last month's rent just to occupy a match-box sized apartment? It taught me not to bump into people without saying, *"excuse me".* That not only is using manners legal, it is also *preferred.*

Marriage is still okay, even if it is not a person.

Hello, I am Shadaria Allison and I am …Married2theMission.

<u>Mission</u>

"You're blessed when you're at the end of your rope. With less of you there is more of God and his rule.

"You're blessed when you feel you've lost what is most dear to you. Only then can you be embraced by the one dearest to you.

"You're blessed when your content with just who you are—no more, no less. That is the moment you find yourselves proud owners of everything that cannot be bought.

"You're blessed when you've worked up a good appetite for God. He is food and drink in the best meal you will ever eat.

"You're blessed when you care. Now of being 'care-full,' you find yourselves cared for.

"You're blessed when you get your inside world—your mind and heart—put right. Then you can see God in the outside world.

"You're blessed when you can show people how to cooperate instead of compete or fight. That is when you discover who you really are, and your place in God's family."

You are blessed when your commitment to God provokes persecution. The persecution drives you even deeper into God's kingdom. -Jesus

Gospel of Matthew 5:3-10 (The Message Version)

"Women if the soul of the nation is to be saved, I believe that you must become its soul".

-Coretta Scott King

♥

History and Hang-up's: *The history of New York City*

Then four great beasts came up out of the sea, each different from
the others. The first beast was like a lion, and it had the wings of
an eagle. I watched until its wings were torn off …
Daniel 7:4 (paraphrased)

HISTORY

I guess it is safe to presume that Great Britain was the "Top Dog" of real estate acquisition in America. Yet, when it came to the north of our beloved, *she-country*, New York, would not be seized without a fight. True to its nature, New York City was a vigilant resistance to all who dared to tame her. Said to be discovered and founded by Giovanni da Verrazano in 1524, the European settlement began with the Dutch in 1609.

Freedom progressed when the proclaimed "Sons of Liberty" finally plotted their disassociation from the dominance of Great Britain's control causing representatives throughout the *Thirteen Colonies to* meet in NYC in 1765 in order to organize their "resistance" to British policy.

After several failed attempts to gain independence through war; featuring *the first president of the United States, George Washington*, New York City succumbed to Great Britain's seizure in 1776. New York City became the home of British militants until 1783 and was the nation's capital until 1790 under the Articles of Confederation that was later replaced with the *United States Constitution*. George Washington's candidacy opened a new life for the city of New York. America welcomed new forums of legislature and laws that would include the drafting of the **United States Bill of Rights**, and the first **Supreme Court of the United States**.

New York City began its life as the *mecca* for business in the 1800's. The Erie Canal gave NYC the ability to trade with outside countries; making NYC a premiere trading location off the Atlantic coast. ***It is amazing the things we can exchange from boats: food, jewelry; people.*** The 18th and 19th century would put NYC on *the map* as one of the most cultured and wealthiest states in the nation. New York openly welcomed both immigrants and the accessibility of its borders as a stand-alone economy boomer surviving both war and the *Great Depression*.

TODAY'S HANGUPS: THE SPIRITUAL CONDITION OF NYC
<u>THE INVISIBLE HAND</u>

Strongholds or "authorities" are often established in fives. Like a human fist, five fingers are needed to grasp hold of any object. The same theory can be demonstrated throughout the territory of any metropolis. In New York City, the strongholds that stagnate growth are obvious: ***idolatry, lust, pride, poverty, and murder.***

Idolatry: Worship of idols. An image or representation of a god used as an object of worship. *(Google Public Data 2018)*

One of the best things about New York City is its ability to market the "cultural melting pot" of our nation. Consequently, ***the worst thing about New York is its ability to market the "cultural melting pot" of our nation.*** This sentiment is especially lived out in the way people worship. I wish I could say that the *Buddha statues* built in the bottom display at my favorite nail salons, or the loud and beautiful Arabic prayer chants from those who practice their religion on various avenues in the morning, were the primitive examples of idolatry in NYC. However, *they are not*.

There are far worse practices of idolatry than we have come to know in New York City; the kind that offer itself to the worship of self, power, fame, and utter darkness.

A Day in the Life of a New Yorker

I was no stranger to public transportation in NYC.

My middle and high school days were filled with *white and green metro card sentiments* of free fares in the city. Even then, I was introduced to the preoccupation people had with themselves. Pushes and shoves through a human-sized turnstile onto the train, glares exchanged from *person to person* when one didn't receive the seat they wanted or the cab *they flagged down before the person standing clearly in front of them, did*; are just some of the *small* examples that lead to far more extreme reflections of the fascination with self. I quietly observed through daily life, that many New Yorkers seemed removed from even the simplest form of compassion towards one another. It was like watching a house full of brothers and sisters who hated one another. I witnessed people *fall* without one person offering to help them up. **I have seen poor people sleep on the floors of stores, churches, and train stations, and kicked from being unseen, or even worse,**

14

ignored. Basic levels of kindness seems up for consideration in NYC.

Though New York is just as beautiful up-close as we see in the movies, the *heroes* of New York are not a part of Marvel or DC comics like those depicted in mainstream cinema. However, if your bank account is on "fleek", your police suit loaded-down with intimidating weaponry, and your name fits just right on the tallest sky rise building, you may be considered "Super-Man" in NYC.

Fame is its own God, power is its throne, and utter darkness has been its consequence. A true centric of the American trademark for all things freedom, New York stands as one of **the most idolatrous cities in the nation**. I suppose with the welcoming exchange of foreign trade relationships, immigration, and its dark ties to westernized religion; it's only right America accommodate everyone's GOD as well.

THE DEFORMATION OF A NATION

THE REBUILDING OF THE TEMPLE OF BAAL IN NYC

I understand hospitality. My stint in the South, granted me the consequence of making people more comfortable than Id ought. However, welcoming people and their God's shouldn't always be a benefit of hospitality.

Pop Quiz:

HOW IS A "CHRISTIAN NATION" PERMITING A REPLICA OF A DEHUMANIZING WITCHCRAFT TEMPLE FROM ANCIENT BABYLONIAN HISTORY TO BE BIRTHED AS A PLACE OF WORSHIP ON AMERICAN SOIL!!!???

Answer:

DON'T.

Baal, commonly known as the most worshiped demon in Phoenician history aside from SATAN, comes to life during the reign of King Ahab (king of the Jews) in the of the Old Testament. A story we can find inside of the most treasured piece of literature in America, the bible.

If we are going to reference ourselves as a country that holds true to the ethic and validity of Christianity, why would we feel at peace erecting a devil worshiping temple in the middle in NYC?

It appears that America believes that the regulation of freedoms; whether by way of opportunities, lifestyle, or the acceptance of people, also means that we can project that same acceptance, spiritually. However, we cannot. If we consider America such a "GOD-FEARING" nation, we need to fasten our beliefs to the GOD who founded our nation as well, and it is certainly NOT Baal. Here is a little food for thought:

Instead of imposing stiff immigration regulations, we can certainly start detoxing our country by kicking the devil out of our own living room.

BACK TO THE MATTER…*at hand*

Lust: A very strong sexual desire.

So that we're being candid, New York City has a *plethora* of good-looking people. After all, mixing some of the most beautiful races derived from various ethnicities, into a sensational and hipster landmass such as NYC; we can expect neck spasms from looking at the beauty coming from every direction. However, we must separate a very natural human attraction to shine a light on a deeper issue, ***the rape victim toll in NYC is at an increasing high.*** According to **NYDAILYNEWS.com**, rape in NYC is an epidemic in 2018. What turns normal attraction to detrimental behavior?

The condition of the heart   and the mind.

Pride: a feeling or deep pleasure or satisfaction derived from one's own achievements, the achievements of those with whom one is closely associated, or from qualities or possessions that are widely admired. The bible advises that the evil that led Satan to lose his glorious seat as the *music ambassador* of heaven, *was his pride*.

It was Satan's erroneous and gluttonous obsession with himself that eventually turned him against God. **New York, is no stranger to the concept of** *pride. Instead it* **inhabits it**. New Yorkers, with our noses in the air, have become a society of *"I make more" and "I look better". This attitude is costing its own people the ability of being heroes in America's story.* After all, what good is the use of glorying in the accomplishments of bribery, inflation of wealth, fame, or glamour, when it all leads to poverty?

Poverty: the state of being extremely poor.

How does one of the highest grossing cities in America become at least half populated in poverty? It is simple: **structuring, classism, racism, and the mistreatment of the poor.** When life is entrenched in impoverished circumstance and the citizens are not at the focal point in a major metropolis, the grievances are far too many to count.

Murder: the unlawful premeditated killing of one human being by another. One of the most gruesome murders I have witnessed in my life was the 2018 televised murder of a 15-year-old young man from the Bronx. *He was murdered at a corner store by five men, almost all of them under 25 years* old. Though murder is capable, both any and everywhere, I do not believe that there is any irony that the murder took place in one of the **most culturally impoverished, crime ridden communities in NYC.**

Since the death of *Lesandra "junior" Guzman Feliz* in the Bronx, the Wall Street Journal has reported murder as "rising" in the year of 2018. Sixty-four percent of the murder rate has increased in the Bronx alone.

Arguably one of the poorest boroughs in NYC, its borders hold the gateway to shelter opportunities which seem for residents to be, no real opportunity at all, as shelters are over flooded.

Captain Obvious **and the clash of the Classes**:
Social deficits and injustices in NYC

Gentrification: *The process of renovating and improving a house or district so that it conforms to middle-class taste.*
2. The process making a person or activity more refined or polite.

Ever go away for a long time and come back to your mom's house and she has all new everything!? I am talking she has moved curtains, family heirlooms, photo albums, dinette sets, *even the cookie jar that she stashed her loose dollars in on the shelf she forbids you to grab from.* That is how I felt when I returned to NYC in 2018.

Nothing was the same.

Sure technology, creativity, and cultural relevancy should be welcomed components of any growing metropolis. However, there is a fine line between improvement and imposing. It was clear upon my arrival in NYC, that the advantage of the ***white and wealthy*** had made its way to some of the fondest urban neighborhoods. Bed-Stuy was now, "Stuyvesant Heights". It seemed Manhattans real estate moved right into Brooklyn. I am not talking downtown, I am talking Crown Heights, and Bed-Stuy; the real "hood" (**and yes, I can share the sentiment, I am from there**). I spent my summers as a child in Marcy *projects* in

Brooklyn, NY, A housing community people ran from in the early 90's. *(Unless you were a Jew with neighboring property)* That same community is now considered prime real estate, now inhabited by *young rich white people.*

Environmental justice has always been a *key culprit by way of* gentrification *throughout America for years.* The *"gag"* has typically been to dissociate the most impoverished communities from resources such as economic development, reputable and efficient healthcare, and education. All while causing division and disparities amongst one social class. This social class is almost ALWAYS the Black and minority communities.

They are treated like animals in cages. Placed near toxic plants, and waste fields. Transferred to the lowest parts of social normalcy, and then eluded to society as monsters. The southern parts of America may have a larger visual sphere of this reality. ***However, New York City is not hiding the agenda of gentrification any better.***

New York, an already expensive living society, masks the requirement of broker fees, and high credit scores to keep the less qualified renters out of nicer neighborhoods (aka MINORITIES). Hiding the accessibility and education of tax abandoned properties and impoverished buildings. Renovating them, and then evicting by circumstance those who both know and make less out of that community.

"My Father's house has many rooms; if that were not so, would I have told you that I am going there to prepare a place for you?"

- John 14:2 NIV

The Fear of Female Leadership in America:
The American Church: *America's Harlot or Heavens Bride?*

Jesus then left the Temple. As he walked away, his disciples pointed out how very impressive the Temple architecture was. Jesus said, "You're not impressed by all this sheer size, are you? The truth of the matter is that there's not a stone in that building that is not going to end up in a pile of rubble." **Matthew 24:1-2**

The American Church has **many secrets**.

Some by which activists and Christian bashers have credible reason to argue the theology of the bible as an incredulous source of doctrine. The American Church exposed by its ties to social corruption, molestation, rape, theft, bribery, and control, was meant to represent the presence of God. Instead, **the American Church has been a corrupted mess of politics, chauvinism, sexism, slavery, demonic initiations, and an all-out WRONG impression of who God is.** We have behaved like a mass of militant and judgmental hypocrites, instead of *the children of an all-loving and encompassing God. Today, we have the nerve to wonder why our country is in disarray.* Even more, we challenge why people in today's culture have begun to cease sitting in our stale-steeped audience.

Why should anyone want to watch our acts of **whore-ism and the popular "pimping" of human emotions at the expense of people's wallets and trust?** Our superior ideals of holiness have been just that, *our ideals of holiness. We have succored to an elite insincerity based on religion and customs aside from an ultimate connection with our creator.*

Help!!! The Bride ran away with the Government

The power of money and need should not share the same place in presence of God. The fundamentals of human character should not be acquainted with power, leadership, or money. It should be shown through in acts of service. Jesus knew that the worries and cares of governmental influence amongst his followers would eventually corrupt them from the inside out. He never intended money to replace his provision.

Tithes and Offerings

Do I believe taking up money to facilitate the matters of the "house" of God is wrong? No. Do I believe it is wrong when it is being astringed from households of *barely making-it-employed people*, YES! Let us define what the matters of God were according to Jesus.

[24] After Jesus and his disciples arrived in Capernaum, the collectors of the two-drachma temple tax came to Peter and asked, "Doesn't your teacher pay the temple tax?"
[25] "Yes, he does," he replied.
"When Peter came into the house, Jesus was the first to speak. "What do you think, Simon?" he asked. "From whom do

the kings of the earth collect duty and taxes—from their own children or from others?"

26 "From others," Peter answered.
"Then the children are exempt," Jesus said to him. 27 "But so that we may not cause offense, go to the lake and throw out your line. Take the first fish you catch; open its mouth and you will find a four-drachma coin. Take it and give it to them for my tax and yours".

(Matthew 17:24-27)

Look and access any of your children young enough to stay at home and ask, how are they able to comfortably pay rent? Not only are they not able… They are not supposed to!

Why is the church purging the pockets of those who can barely afford to pay their bills? They show up to the house of God being asked to sow into a miracle or a breakthrough or the "fees" of the church. A structure that does not even make itself available for a full twenty-four hours. A building virtually unavailable to the sleeping homeless person on its front steps. Simply put, the church is in danger ethically.If we do not teach the fallacy of religious custom and the free offering of Christ synonymously, then we are trespassing the human right for the truth and causing the Gospel to be questionable. We should not be surprised when people walk away or challenge what we believe in when we say we are Christians.

There is by no circumstance that the mission of the church, which is to fundamentally build people, community, and world; able to complete that mission if those who are supposed to work and serve there are the same ones compensating its very own facility.

In this country, there is an emphasis on the separation of church and state but how can that be when we rely heavily on the work and the *brand* of Christianity and its church

Some of the reasons that we have lost out credibility in America is because of our lack of mobility.

There needs to be something in the law that provides the church movement with guaranteed funding.

I can assure you that it would reduce the need for government assistance and the need for government reliance.

The church should receive the funding because we also should be charged with the responsibility of taking care of the community. Instead, the pastors are getting rich from poor members who can barely keep their lights on, when we have as system of government in place that can help with that.

"A religion that is pure and stainless according to God the Father is this: to take care of orphans and widows who are suffering, and to keep oneself unstained by the world." -James 1:27

We have exchanged the intention of the tithe, for the greed of possession and personal gain. It has become a stench before God.

GOD IS NOT PLEASED.

Jesus created examples of his intention for giving every time he shared the gospel with the poor while feeding people.

He knew that any other need for the world's economy would drive a sense of reliability and idolatry for money. One that would conflict with soul's need for God himself.

"What good will it be for someone to gain the whole world, yet forfeit their soul? Or what can anyone give in exchange for their soul?"
-Matthew 16:26

He was very careful how he conveyed the uses of money. The original tithe was a test of hearts for the Levitical priesthood; pre-Christ, or those who lived in the temple and did not work like other Jewish citizens. (Full Story in Malachi 3)

Tithing and offerings in today's church has become nothing more than a "cash cow" for appearances. In some fellowships, tithing has been used to commercialize the "haves from the have nots. People have been so influenced by its power that they believe they can buy comradery and even worse, love and forgiveness from God. The entire idea of the tithe and the offering was to both test the will and to aid in the community. Anything outside of that, we should all question.

Deep! Real deep.

Male Dominance and Control in the American Church

I loved going to church as a child. Every Sunday I was filled with this unyielding desire to know God. I'd come in and try my best to sit super close to the front so that I could feel his presence. Somehow, I thought that by being closer to the pulpit, Id meet God there. To my surprise, I would be told to move back three rows because the first row was designated for the *first lady* and her attendants. Then there were the armor bearers, pastor's children, and a special spot left open at the end of the front row, *just in case there was a guest speaker*. I quickly learned that there was much to learn about God's house. *Much to learn indeed.*

Often reflecting on the landscapes of various churches Id visited, I noticed the obvious differences between the male and the female attendees. All around the church, I'd see women. Women on the usher board, women in the choir, women bringing announcements, women working in the nursery, women everywhere. **Everywhere, but the pulpit.** Women made great servants in the church.

They were timely and loyal. Laboring tirelessly, whether it were on service projects, cooking in the kitchen, or in prayer. Women were indeed the oil of the machine called, the church; **especially the black church.**

The pastor often seemed honored above the spouse. The stench of coursed loyalty, seemed almost cultic. There was a commonality of male in the pulpits preaching but the women remained in subservient roles. *The first time I heard a female preach, it changed my life.* There was a depth of strength found in the voice of that woman. It was so different, refreshing even.

It was a much needed break from the repetitious grander of the "elite baritone" week after week.

I don't know if I was more impressed from her intellect or the fact that her presence there, was like a rebuttal to the traditional church structure.

A structure that seemed to send a subliminal message, which placed women; all of them, in subservient roles, instead of leadership. This left open for the interpretation, a subtle misconception that women were spiritually subservient to men, and that it should be granted only by special circumstance, that the female voice be heard by the congregation.

Some pastors would even elude in sermons that the female input was out of place in the church and that the *word of God supported the absence of female engagement during service.*

For God is not a God of confusion but of peace. As in all the churches of the saints, the women should keep silent in the churches. For they are not permitted to speak, but should be in submission, as the Law also says. If there is anything they desire to learn, let them ask their husbands at home. For it is shameful for a woman to speak in church. (1 COR 14:33-35)

This passage found in the bible seems to jump off the pages of biblical scripture and into the rule book of leaders around the world.

Paul of Damascus, coined as the glorified "convert" of the New Testament, was an orthodox Jew who murdered Christians before his conversion to Christianity.

As believers in Christ, we go through transformations in our character as we relate deeper with God. The Holy Spirit, through a process called *sanctification.* A process believers experience while merging with Christ, by which takes our old mindsets, behaviors, and beliefs through a metamorphosis, in order to align more with Yeshua (Jesus).

Taking this into account, it is safe to presume that some of the legalistic, self-righteous, chauvinism that reeked from Paul's statement came from a very religious and limited perspective point in his process of sanctification.

Some of the best teachers of the word unto this day are women. It is a shame that there are some churches out there, who are robbing the world blind of the wisdom that is naturally welcomed by the female voice. The way is saw it then and the way I still see it now is all the same. If we are good enough to breed, smart enough to aid, loved enough to marry, and daring enough to carry civilization from the dawn of eternity until now, why aren't women qualified to administer the truths of the scriptures?

The woman has had an indefinite target on her back since her infamous fall in the Garden of Eden. (Full story available in Genesis of Bible) Even until today, she has been discredited amongst the world; devoid of her original value and ridiculed amongst society as the mere prize of man. She has been found lacking her true essence as man's best partner. When God laid the plan out for the worlds order. God advised that it wasn't good for man to be alone and that his helper, the woman was the best partner for him to keep watch over creation. Since then, the world has neglected this fact and the evidence is certain. **There is no system in place that can be successfully run without the equal balance of female insight**. **It is time to trash the traditions.** God made man (humans) in his image to execute his glory. It is God's impartial love and agenda for human beings, by design to live in complete commune with him. **When God fashioned women,** *it was NEVER his intention to limit her as a silent domesticated machine with a lack of ideas or opinions.* Instead, God solidified her importance by placing her at the genesis of creation. He fashioned her from the rib of a man to aid in his purpose, and to birth God's entire population.

Not a soul on earth would be here without her.

I believe it is the realization of that fact, which blinds the male of her importance and intimidated the enemy. As long as men and women hate one another, the devil wins. **The woman has been perpetually stripped of her God-given authority; first in ministry, next in society, and especially in America.**

<u>FATHER JEZEBEL</u>

There are history books filled with several descriptions on how Christianity was used against blacks in America. We can no longer as a sound country deny the injustice committed to the African American people. We just cannot. Being beaten, taken from their home, enslaved, raped, humiliated, castrated, and then imprisoned with the same book that in fact *guaranteed their freedom*. A temple was built and became more of a political safe house against brutal racism than an actual house for the lords dwelling. Their faith won over their oppression and the blacks ultimately created a haven around the church. Even there, they were attacked. Private deals and meetings with those who ran the occult practices partnered with some and then in other forms the church was invaded by white euphemists who were "blood thirsty" savages, aiming only to destroy the African American at all costs. Even if it meant killing them and attacking them in one of the only safe places they knew, the church. *I have seen Jezebel wear more suits and beards then she has skirts and make up.*

"Nevertheless, I have this against you: You tolerate that woman Jezebel, who calls herself a prophet. By her teaching she misleads my servants into sexual immorality and the eating of food sacrificed to idols." -Revelation 2:20

Infamous for idolatry, HO-ism, (and yes, I said HO-ism) and devil worship, Jezebel (the evil queen who worshiped Baal) has taken the wrap for representing every sexy, beautiful, godly, ungodly, pretty, holy, hood-rat, upscale, business, ethical, un-ethical, *woman in the world*. The most dominant female villain mentioned in the bible, Jezebel was a Phoenician seductress married to King Ahab of Israel. Jezebel was a witch of a Queen, who agitated and murdered the voice and the people of Yahweh (God of Israel) and his chosen prophets. Her weapons of choice were seduction, control, manipulation, and **"by domination of the spiritually and emotionally vulnerable"**. She is the culprit of several deceitful crimes and occult practices throughout her short-lived physical reign in biblical history. As a malicious protagonist of the demonic, Jezebel is famous for intimidating Gods prophet, Elijah, by threatening his life. In vengeance of his people, God encourages Elijah from hiding from her and uses Elijah to serve notice to Jezebel; that her days were numbered in the kingdom, and that justice would prevail at the price of her own blood. She is ultimately denied of her power, thrown unto her death and eaten by dogs. (Full story available in 2 Kings of the Bible)

What does this have to do with the Modern American Church?

As with any event of human death, the spirit remains. Jezebel's ties to the demonic worship of Baal, (the devil) point to a deeper agenda that is very much alive today; both in the church, and in America. The operation of occult dominance, the manipulation of feeble or disadvantaged minds, the assassination of those who are influenced by God to tell his truth, and the bondage of idolatry, all seep into what we know as "GOD and Country" present day America. Ironically, women have not had the privilege in a position of power long enough to host; past an opinionated senate; or a 45-minute sermonette on *Women's Sunday*. Yet and still, because we have the option of skirt or pant, concealer, liner, or bare face; we are instantly coined after Jezebel herself. A woman can go to school, manage a corporate business, and still not be worthy of leadership without the premise of doubt in her capabilities.

If a woman has an "eruption" from the spirit of God in a church setting or in life, and is engaged by his call of her to minister the gospel, she is questioned as one who forsook her role in society, as a domestic courier. One "buck" against the male-matrix of systemic control, and the woman is then seen as nothing more than a manipulative, emotional, and power driven, "Jezebel". The woman; never truly having a place to destroy; yet destruction is all around her.

Never having a voice beyond domestication, yet told to submit. Advised that a moment in time with her leading; would mean the demise of a nation and the disgrace of all things holy or patriotic. 2018 has ended. America is still in turmoil. The church structure is in an all-out threat of collapse in its influence. Without a woman in charge of it all.

Look around AMERICA!! There are MEN EVERYWHERE at the PERFERBIAL "top", and the dogs are hungry; Yet again.

IF JESUS IS THE SECOND ADAM…
THE "CHURCH" IS THE SECOND EVE.

THE CHURCH IS THE BRIDE OF AMERICA.

WOMEN ARE NEEDED AT THIS TIME.
ALWAYS HAVE BEEN.
ALWAYS WILL BE.

TREAT US AS SUCH.

"The woman was given the two wings of a great eagle, so that she might fly to the place prepared for her in the wilderness, where she would be taken care of for a time, times and half a time, out of the serpent's reach."

-Revelation 12:14

Black Woman Blues: "History of Horror" 4 "Future Glory"

When it came down to beauty, film, standard; or anything that involved women in the limelight, Black women in this country were regarded nothing more than silhouettes; faded shadows behind porcelain images of perfection found as mere dust amongst those who held the most power, *white America.*

So, what is a woman to do if she is black, beaten, and forced into a "homeland" where she has no home? She lives in sorrow, is imprisoned, denied, degraded, and dreaded. The various slave and racial crimes committed throughout American history are surmountable. They are at best, under-regarded by some and forgotten by far too many. However, there is no hiding that slavery's grueling effects are felt in present day America.

Black Pearl Faces in a White Oyster of American Culture

When you treat humans like property, the results are horrific.

The black woman was a "goldmine" in early America, mainly *because her baby meant more free labor*. From the genesis of this nation, the black woman has been regarded as a mere pawn in the creation of more slaves. ***Slaves do the work of those in power***. Back then, it didn't matter who bred with her, the black woman just needed to produce more slaves in America. , Whether it happened with white or black men, the canal of the black woman was exploited for life. Her seed was regarded only valuable in the matters of creating bondage-d men and women. What a horrible reality. Imagine the psychosis the human mind could take on if it were made to believe that its total existence, was based on devaluation and rape. This has been the perpetual reality of the **BLACK WOMAN in America.**

To be a black woman in this country, meant to be deemed only good enough to produce, often good enough to have some rare stranger invade your body, cycle after cycle ; never having the luxury to attach yourself to the baby growing in your womb because it was often the product of illegitimate discrepancy. **What an unpaid PRICE to pay.**

The black woman living as a slave in America, seemed like a life sentence to live in a state of brokenness. Your husband, if you were allowed to have one; was sold for labor. You were separated from your own mate to breed with your slave master, or else you where whipped into working cotton fields.

Your baby was considered as good as a stranger because as a black woman you were required to feed the entire culture off of your breast. This meant you fed the white oppressor's child well before; if at all your own child. These things were all carried out, without the ability to fight back; because fighting back as a black woman in America, would cost you your life.

As time catapulted us throughout history, the Black woman seemingly gets her chance at "bought freedoms".

She becomes more and more alive to the fact that she is not as beautiful as her counterpart, the white woman. She is not allowed the knowledge of beauty technique to make herself more attractive. This realization brings about a traumatic sense of self-image. The black woman's life is not her own. She is depraved, taunted, and raped. Her hair is coiled. Her lips are full. Her hips are wide. Her eyes are dark. Her skin is Black. She is called a "monkey", she is called a "Nigger" she is labeled as an outcast in a place she built, both by hand and mind. **No one ever thinking to tell her that she was the mother of an entire nation.**

If numbers could ever be calculated about how much the black woman should be paid for birthing an entire civilization, we may have to create a new planet to fund both her and her people.

For that, America should be most grateful. At the dusk of discovering the value of her existence, the black woman becomes a variant of all things. Black women become activists, actresses, theater majors, students, council women, scholars, and astronauts.

She goes on to influence society in media and beauty, economics, and social sciences.

The black woman becomes a living miracle to the nation she birthed because what once was inaccessible to her; she begins to not only influence but dominate. Seldom receiving any credit for all she does, somehow the soul of the black woman presses on. All while understanding that in order to gain any sense of normalcy, she must almost the impossible. She must succeed.

The social breakthrough of the Black woman, would not be televised. Facebook, Instagram, or twitter were nonexistent. There was only prayer, fighting, and a UN yielding pursuit of legacy driven freedom. What black women did throughout the history in America was nothing short of remarkable. The sufferings of her day opened the doors for the present day "Millennial Generation" without argument, and very little acknowledgement from the country at all.

Black Butterfly: The evolution of "mother nation"

I was born on September 3, 1986. A product of what some may consider the "drug era". I lived and am living in a history of remarkable change. Fast forwarding through the times of pin curls, afros, and Shirley temples, I was birthed into the "French roll and "finger waved" door-knocking earring rocking" … "Cross colored wearing", "poetic justice braided", *Millennial Generation.*

In between food stamps and section 8 living, I had not a care in the world. When life got hard, I had my friends, cousins, CHURCH and
"OooOOOOOO…on the TLC tip". My mamma was a beast in the working industry. She had about six jobs, not because she wanted too, but because she had too; if we were going to have a decent living. My mom raising me a single mother, was a norm in my childhood society. Amongst those in my neighborhood, we all looked the same. Mamma working, daddy not around. Never would I have imagined while flipping cartwheels, and dancing in mirrors with my hand on one hip that I would have any part in the history beyond the urban living I saw.

I would have never thought that while catching lighting bugs, and watching TGIF on ABC network television; or that while reading "The Babysitters Club" and watching "All that" on "Snick" that I would have any voice or any care about the history that I was living in.

Welfare was not well...fair.

The supposed resolve to ending poverty, was also the birthing of welfare. As a child, and even well into my adult years, I had to play the game of "Governmental assistance".

Do not misinterpret what I am about to say because I truly believe that the help served as a staple for my family. However, its stench was the glaringly obvious target towards a more specific demographic, *the black woman.*

In most cases, to qualify you had to be a single mother with one or more children, no father in the household or very limited resources. At best, you could own an *opinion and a bus pass.* Anything more than that, and you were on your own.

The state-employees treated you like you were *"Orphan Oliver";* even if you were employed by McDonald's, your tax dollar contribution didn't qualify you to be treated well. Families were given an endless surplus of food stamps, and a limited supply of cash or other quintessential resources to function in society.

The government was ensuring our survival, but at the expense of the knowledge needed for us as black women taking care of our families to thrive. Welfare put a Band-Aid on a flood throughout the black communities because without the education of how to both save and acquire money, black people; especially women, were at a deficit, left only with a glorified "handout" from the government. All at once, black women went from the cotton fields, to the governments system. A tragic reality.

At the birthing of what is perceived as a new Dawn, the black and Latino woman have made a massive progression. We have fought our way through government obscurity, environmental injustice, and systemic poverty. We have gone on to lead in this nation, yet with limited authority or appreciation. We have begun to engineer small business, yet with limited access to fair funding, and we have gone on to attempt to run this nation, yet without fairness in strategy, funding, or legitimate democracy. With all due respect we deserve more. Our men deserve more, and our children deserve a fair chance at generational wealth and freedom.

Though my plight is for all women from all colors and backgrounds, there has been no treatment, neither will there ever be another like the mistreatment of the black woman and man in America.

Latinos, America's "New Nigg$#"

I love Latin America. All heritages, all colors, all ethnicities, all demographics. The example they are to the world, is one to be patterned after. We have been blessed to be surrounded by these beautiful people. While living in Birmingham, I witnessed the mistreatment of the Hispanic community on deep social levels.

I would witness men line up every morning to take a van. There would be at least 17 men at one stop waiting to load up to go to a construction job.

They opted to take a working van over the unreliable bus transportation offered in the city. They were often taunted by the public. People whispered about them amongst themselves, and paid them the smallest they could make because they were seen as desperate to live under the freedoms of America.

As times went on, I noticed more Mexicans working in fast food restaurants around town.

I often admired their work ethic and undying loyalty to their families. Though they saw other people mocking them and talking about how they cleaned or how they looked, I saw the persistence and diligence like those of my own culture in the African American culture. Under what seemed to be a glaring sense of scrutiny, the Hispanics preserved their own economy by living in smaller apartments with larger groups of people, even in the acquisition of owning their own businesses.

It quickly dawned on me that the Latin community had become the "new negro". Hands to build, hearts to learn, and sadly; another force to sabotage. Contributing much to the social construct of this nation, yet lacking true acceptance from the American people.

Latin American Women: God's Secret Weapon

HBO was so important to my childhood entertainment.

Weekends in my adolescent years consisted of *Tostitos' branded* cheese pizza, a glass of juice, and big eyes glued to *"Selena",* a powerful biopic about a female Mexican superstar, starring the beautiful Jennifer Lopez. Watching Selena was the first time I was able to co-relate the minority struggle through the eyes of those who seemed to not be so different than me; Latin American women.

The summer of 2013 re-invigorated that sentiment, during a visit to a local laundromat owned by a Mexican woman. After washing a few loads of clothing, we discussed her story. She told me she was an immigrant from Mexico that decided that her and her family needed a better life. Together they put both, their hands and dollars into her dream of opening a laundromat, here in America.

Obviously succeeding in that goal, she was happy to own real estate in a flourishing community in the Deep South. As I watched and listened to her eagerly express how important it was for her people to learn work, appreciate, and co-exist in what has been deemed as the 'free world", I heard the heartbeat of my own people.

I wondered where the hatred for these people began in our country. After all, the land was once theirs as well. The Treaty of Guadalupe Hidalgo in 1848, which was supposed to offer the peace and the exchange of their own ship of land in America, proves that maybe they didn't have an issue in our land. Maybe they were just coming back home. Mexicans used to own a portion of America. This is their home.

Over time, I began to see more and more businesses, grocery stores, real estate, and restaurants grow and run at the leadership of Latin American women. Their determination to win, by building together with their family is like none I have ever seen. They understood the importance of equipping themselves with enough unity to become a profitable addition; even to a place that wanted nothing to do with them at all. Much like, my people.

Today, Latin American women have been a force to be reckoned with. Dominating in pop culture; as Cardi-B and others have been celebrated by the country as innovators and passionate artists. Latin American women have joined the culture as rising leaders.

With bold new faces of leadership such as Alexandria Ocasio-Cortez, who in 2018, took the seat at only 29 as the youngest woman to ever serve in the U.S. House of Representatives.

The nation is undoubtedly adopting an influx of the Latin American people and I believe it is a good growth to this land, and we should not fear the help that they can and do present this country. America could honestly stand to learn a thing or two about the values of culture and family heritage from them.

To witness the devastating racism and horror stories that have come from the building of wall and the separation of Hispanics from their families, has the stench of Early American supremacy all over it. It all reminds me of how Black people were painted in cinema and in the culture as threats and savage to American society, awhile barely laying a finger to anyone and while over extending labor, ideas, and life to a nation that hated them from the beginning.

I remember speaking to a group of teenagers at Bethel High school once in Virginia. There was a Spanish young lady in tears behind being taunted for her heritage and the fight of her people at the border of a country made up in its entirety by immigrants. What exactly are we teaching our country? That white is right? That immigrants are the enemy? Or what we really need to admit on a cultural level. That we are afraid. We live a life in constant fear of someone taking over our **possessions, killing our people, and terrorizing our nation. Just like we did to get the very land we occupy. Shame on us. We need to repent.**

"He makes sure that orphans and widows are treated fairly; he loves the foreigners who live with our people, and gives them food and clothes. So then, show love for those foreigners, because you were once foreigners in Egypt."(Deuteronomy 10:18-19)

Bloody Feathers: *A tribute to Native American Women*

I cannot imagine the bribe
The fear found from tribes
I do not know the pain
Of what happened to this soil
When you died
You are a nation
A chosen Generation your bloody sacrifice often
disregarded
Treating your homeland like a vacation.
I salute you
Through stone I will never know
When I see braids down to elderly woman's ankles
Colored black as night or white as snow
You're hunted with men, ran with the rain
Your race is legendary; in this country filled with pain you sustain; your
courage lives on through centuries of varied weather your beauty regal
On a land stained
All over the place...beautiful
Bloody Feathers
-Shadaria Allison

Color Me Paid
Racial bias and structured pay amongst women

As a little girl, I remember people telling the infamous jokes that carried the unforgettable introduction of...

"There was a White guy, a Black guy, and a Latino guy."

Somehow, the handles at the end of these race-driven jokes were positioned in a way that always employed minorities as come up as the "butt" of the joke. Some say there is always some element of truth to a joke. As the American economy still surrenders minority earnings as some of the lowest in national averages.

To put it plainly:

WHITE MALES ARE THE HIGHEST PAID IN AMERICA.

Acknowledging that America is a country founded upon greed, gain, and racial supremacy, we stand now at the end of an era asking our government; *can we all just get our fair share*? After all, what difference should color, or sex *really* make; if there are two or more persons with the same capabilities, competency, and work ethic, doing the same job, at the same time, for the same employer? It is past our time to adjust the way we fund this economy. These structures were put in place, so that the minority would forever run the "hamster's wheel" into systemic poverty.

Our economy in all its stagnant, *yet seemingly progressive glory* needs to rid itself of some racist and chauvinistic values. The averages from economic statistics confirm that the White male in America is bringing home seven more dollars than the White female. The Black male is bringing home two more dollars than the black female. The Hispanic male are bringing home almost three dollars more than the Hispanic female. **AMERICA, WE GOT SOME EXPLAINING TO DO!!!!!!!!!!**

On June 10, 1963, America established what is called **the Equal Pay Act**, a United States labor law that abolished the wage disparity based on sex. In 2017, I started a petition to call the Presidents attention to the fact that this law has been ultimately ignored. Not only for women but for minorities. Though I gained over 100 signatures (the required minimum via change.org) I still received no response from the president. If America were to determine pay based on the worth of a person, these figures suggest that people are intentionally paid based on color and gender, rather than what they are truly worth. This is beyond sad and it's wrong. What then are we communicating to our growing culture? We are telling our country that we are more interested in the dominance of White America, rather than that of equality for all Americans. **The arguable reality is that the best of America's workforce is made up in the majority by minority women. A fact well known in America; both past and future.** As even the POTUS tapped on the shoulder of an African American female in 2016, to grant some form of administration in the White House.

The asset of the minority female in this country is invaluable.

The asset of the female in this country period, is necessary

66

CHURCHES take up a profound amount of real estate throughout local communities. Can we not consider their conversion into multi-functional Rehab and Recreational facilities? Even at possible...a HOSPITAL?

SHADARIA ALLISON,
FOUNDER OF
MARRIED2THEMISSION

www.shadariaallison.com

www.shadariaallison.com

IG: Married2themission

Married2theMission: New York City
Part A: Married2theMission
Part B: Rehabilitation and Recreation

Married2theMission is a MOVEMENT of Lady Advocates, united to promote the reconstruction of faith-based organizations by way of deliberate partnerships with healthcare industry professionals, and the adjustment of governmental infrastructures in order to serve real communal needs.

I wrote President Trump in 2016. I was given the idea by a total stranger in a soul food restaurant in Birmingham, AL. I spent hours telling her about my passion for the impoverished, drug addicted, and mentally ill community in our metropolis, and my *big dream* to turn one of the local dilapidated hospital structures into a state-of-the-art recreational and rehabilitation facility for the city.

Upon his election, Trump elected Ben Carson to lead over the urban housing development in America. I figured that his hand coupled with my myriad of natural talent and passion for the community, would serve to fund the initiative.

Lofty dreams for a woman without resources, credit, a degree and zero credentials. With the growing homeless rate, the developing continuation of violence, depression, and poverty. I did not see why the idea was a bad one. So, without any money or connections I remember sending him my professional biography with a letter enclosed. I told him that even though he wasn't the nation's most favorable choice, that Id stand in prayer for him. I also offered him a bit of advice to win the hearts of the people.

I advised him that participating in initiatives that reflected the vital needs of the local community would more than likely give him an upper hand in his candidacy. I strongly felt that in showing America he had a heart for reformation, and the prosperity of its people beyond typical *republican political perspective*; would change America's views of him.

Of course, I heard nothing back. This would not stop my determination as the will to see reform for the "least of these" pushed me to write my first book: **Married2TheMission**: **Birmingham, a City Destined for Reform.**

The book would be less than 100 pages, detailed with a plan that offered a way to introduce communal reform on a comprehensive level. I offered a layout that would include how the effects of poverty, racism, and violence had caused an influx of poverty and criminal activity in Birmingham, AL., and how with the willingness to combine faith based communities (churches) hospitals, and local municipalities to come together to fund a state-of-the-art Recreational and Rehab facility, we could stand to turn the city, and perhaps even the state towards a "breakthrough".

My goal: To make this happen in every state in America.

Shadaria A. Allison: From homeless to author to film cameo with Queen Latifah

By **Birmingham Times** - April 12, 2018   👁 1566   💬 0

 Facebook  Twitter

Shadaria Allison. (Provided Photo)

By Je'Don Holloway Talley
For the Birmingham Times

The idea was a "hit" as it pertained to local publicity. I was published in the local Birmingham newspaper, and WBRC Fox News 6 television. People who witnessed most of my works in local community service, rallied towards the idea of featuring me as a budding author.

Local radio stations jumped at the opportunity to showcase a young woman with such a passion for the community.

Yet, there was no real response from people who could make the better difference economically and so my cry fell on deaf ears.

I thought to market my book as a "creative campaign" of sorts, I hoped to see the initiative go the "distance". **I knew I did not have the money. I knew I did not have the credit.** I knew I did not **know the right people, but I tried**. I gave the greater portion of the book away to every homeless person I could find in Birmingham.

I had a fancy book signing at the Birmingham Civil Rights Foot soldiers Headquarters downtown, in hopes to raise enough money to fund the campaign project. I showed up at community meetings. I spoke with local reformists who "spear headed "other communal assignments, yet to no avail. With no support, money, or anyone to invest beyond public accolade, I went back to my original idea.
I mailed President Trump two copies of the book.

As I will do with this one, and everyone until I reach him personally.

Rehabilitation and Recreation

I will never forget interviewing on Fox 6 about Married2theMission.

After my publicist prepped me, I walked into the studio and the newscaster began asking me a series of questions concerning the book. I was well into the middle of my interview on national stream and local broadcasting outlets, with the realization that I was "live"; until the interviewer asked me the most prolific questions about my goals for the book.

After expressing that I envisioned Caraway, an historic dilapidated hospital located in central downtown Birmingham becoming a state of the art rehabilitation and recreational facility catering to both the immediate and prolonged needs of the mentally ill, drug addicted, and homeless citizens of the Birmingham community, he wanted to know something more.

"But you're talking locally how to make these changes," He said.

 "Is this a model for elsewhere as well?

"Oooh …look at you". I replied.

"Sort of", I replied. "I think that there needs to be a rehabilitation and recreational facility in every state and eventually every country."

Before I knew it, the three years of journaling M2M on every state in the back of my Calendars and notebooks, flooded my memory. What the newscaster was not privy too, was my bigger desire. I loved Birmingham and wanted to see it be the nucleus of reformation, but the vision that ached my soul was much bigger. The vision that moved me was for more than a city, it was for my country. **It was for America**. Watching the stifling death tolls in America average over 80 percent in 2018, harboring at its core, issues like depression, mental illness, mass shootings, and hatred, all reminded me that I was not exactly "dreaming" too big and that what I had in mind, may have been perfectly aligned with the heartbeat of God.

There is not a state, place, or person today that could not benefit from rehabilitation and recreation. **I believe NYC has the resources to back the project and to influence its need throughout the rest of our nation**.

I believe it holds the power to execute on a global level and to truly aid in the progression of innovative thinking that will charter our nation as a stand-alone beacon of hope for the rest of the world.

Rehabilitation, by several definitions, **is the deliberate action of restoring people to health or normalcy through various methods of training and therapy after remarkable trauma; not limited to imprisonment, addiction, or illness.** Recreation can be defined as **the activity done for enjoyment when people not working for the benefits of wellness and personal growth.**

Like any other human who has gone through life, we all know that there are various experiences that leave us in dire need of both elements. Where mental illness and other forms of addiction and stressors where once seen as conversational "taboo" they are now as common as zipping up a coat.

As our current culture adjusts to the normalcy of vast change, and in some cases various forms of social and cultural dysfunction accompanied by this change.
It is imperative; now more than ever that we establish reliable sources of help to our people. First on a national level, then on a global one.

Operation Church

 I remember watching the movie, *End of Days* with my dad at a NYC movie theater with my dad as a child. I hated being scared, but I remember observing this movie and I would have a noticeable commonality. Whenever the main character of the movie got into a peak of terror and was found on the run, or seeking to find credible advice, a place to hide, or any other wisdom on what to do in times of trouble; even when there were climatic action-packed "chase" scene, I took notice to one thing in particular, *all the victims ran to the church.*

The church has historically been a valued staple throughout the communities of America. No matter what denomination or direct belief, this country has had a history of being grounded through the Christian church.
Even as a young girl, I assumed that when I went to church everything was going to be better. Whether it was the spark of a smiling greeter, an inspiring word from a charismatic pastor, or *even a full belly from the bottom of the church kitchen.* The church, was always a place that I expected to find safety
It was the one place expected to house holiness, peace, and above all else, the presence of God. Though I did not have any visible killers or demons chasing after me like the ones in the movies, I recognized that it was the presumed responsibility of the church to be one of the safest places on earth.

Today, I'm sad to say; not so much.

Before I expound on the ways I feel that the American church has fallen short of both the representation and the mandate of Christ, I want to say too, in its defense, that **there is no other remedy beyond Christ as an advocate for humanity besides the church. Church as in the people.**
Church by its very definition is reference as; a body of believers. However, when I mention todays "church" I am mentioning its existence as a much needed authority in this nation. I will not appease the ears of men or women to say that the church is a place where we may continue to grow comfortable as "the friendliest place on earth".

I am afraid we are in a different time. The church must be what it once was; a body of believers moving in unison and power under the authority of God to aid, help, assistance, and save community.

Having benefited directly from the gathering of like-minded believers in various assemblies all of my life, I understand the climate of America, and the change of gears the church must take in present history. In light of that understanding, I know that just as we hold dear to the importance of electing different governmental officials, in order to legislated provide the policies that reforms and aid in securing the future of our country, we must submit that same tenacity in initiating, funding, and resourcing the reformation of the American church.

WE MUST BEGIN TO ESTABLISH THE KINGDOM OF HEAVEN ON EARTH AS IT IS IN HEAVEN; IN LIFESTYLE, DEED, ETHIC, AND RESOURCING.

If we do not, we are in danger of losing; not just a harvest of believers, but **our very nation**.

Gone are the days when we can hand out flyers and petition social media "lives" and various posts to do the collective work of the church. We are now in a time where we will have to both "fish" and aid the people. The waters are murky, and the tides are high but our promissory position in heaven is not the only one to gain.

God is interested in the foreigner, the stripper, the government, the rich, the poor, the stripper, the businessmen, the celebrity, the man, the woman, the child, the criminal, the lonely, the depressed, the drug addicted, the mentally ill, the suicidal teen, and the homeless. He's interested in the world. **The world we know here in our nation and then in the world.** I wish I could say that technology advancements and small groups an all organized carnival-like strategies formally employed by the church are still beneficial, but they are not. The thing that we Americans and people all over the world are looking to get truly healed from is detrimental *inner illness.* **When people are detrimentally ill, they must go to the hospital.**

What better hospital than the church?

"When Jesus heard this, he said, "Healthy people don't need a doctor-sick people do"
- Mark 9:12

It is my belief that every church that claims to be a facilitator of the gospel of Jesus Christ should be a major operational facility. All of them; opened to the public, staffed, and accessible 24 hours a day.

The passive understanding that when people gather in the halls of the church, it is merely to do some ceremonial song and dance, coupled with a few hours of preaching and community service, is in its extreme; **devoid of the original response to the Gospel.**

If we are going to be people who are said to be replicating the teachings and understandings of the Bible, then we must get a little deeper than that. When we observe the practices of Christ outside of his normal participation in the Jewish custom and festivities, we observe and often celebrate the life of a die-hard humanitarian who was readily available. Available to help people with hard things. Whether it was the provision of power, food, word, service, supply, or healing, he was a man found on the move.

On foot alone, Jesus was a rehabilitation and recreational facility.

Knowing this, I try to wrap my head around the ordinance of the building structures made available today called "churches" being anything less. If we must condense the understanding of what the church means to the entire world to the confines of a building, then it is time we become a useful one.

Married2The Mission

If money were not an issue, and it should not be, considering the millions of dollars that rotate in and out of churches on any given Sunday. Oh, and before I forget, the partial ownership by our government due to the acquisition of the 501 c3 status here in America. We should have the funding indeed.

I envision creating a network of women that advocate and implement the building of state-of-the-art dormitory styled recreation and rehabilitation facilities with both Christ at the Center, and the community as its focus.

This initiative will require extensive partnerships and collaborations with healthcare professionals, educators, community organizers, and government participation at both the federal and the state levels; as we would also like to cut the governmental labors in half, by facilitating a great deal of communal needs through the church. A cry that has been overlooked and necessary in a time such as this.

To produce this initiative, we will need a whole lot of help, and a whole lot of God. When in service of communal reform, especially as it pertains to people who have struggled with mental illness, drug addiction, and homelessness, you will need more than over spiritualized and ritualistic regimens. We will need hands. The hands of doctors and healthcare specialists that can properly diagnose and treat various ailments.

We will need the help of psychologists, counselors, and educators that can help extend comprehensive rehabilitation plans for those in need. We will also be in need of physical trainers, dietary specialists.

We will need social workers to aid with abused women, runaways, mentally ill, and homeless victims. We will also require administrators who can execute temporary recreation and housing development plans. This will open up employment in this country on levels this nation have never seen. We will need ministers who can clearly intertwine advancing the Gospel, while actively aiding people with the application of the love of God. This will take philanthropy and service. It will change the way we do "church" forever. **It is time for there to be legislative initiatives that give power to the principles of the kingdom, and not just the supremacy of our country.** This operation would need the cooperation of three realms of power.

"For the kingdom of God is not a matter of eating and drinking, but of righteousness, peace and joy in the Holy Spirit."
Romans 14:17

The Government:

Our constitution advises that there must be a separation between church and state. However, majority of today's American churches are 501 C-3 organizations functioning under the federal control of the government. I am not a scholar in the matter, but I believe that warrants them both parties to ask and receive money under Governmental rule, and if needed; its seizure. If this is so, there needs to be some form of revision submitted to the way religious organizations are funded and protected by the government, if we are to remain under its influence.

If so, then it should be funded undoubtedly, by the same.

There also needs to be some availability to market this plan to America's biggest economic influencers, i.e.: Athlete's, law makers, banks, celebrities, and Tax-Payers. The more responsibility the church takes on, the more it should be provided. If we are going to work around the clock as a church body, we are going to need legislative power, monetary resource, and national help.

Health Care Professionals:

If we are able to reform the American church into state of the art rehab and recreational facilities, we will in no doubt need to hire several health care professionals. These doctors will need to have specialized in drug rehabilitation care, mental healthcare, psychiatry, family counseling, and a range of other medical expertise. We would need a genuine part of the facility to run as a small functioning hospital. I believe this would create a ton of new jobs for health care professionals.

"On hearing this, Jesus said to them, "It is not the healthy who need a doctor, but the sick. I have not come to call the righteous, but sinners."
Mark 2:17

Faith Based Communities- "The Church"

The truth of the matter is that the church has, even with its many flaws, been a VITAL pillar in American history.
For my people in particular, it was a hedge of protection from racial euphemists who never intended to see God in us.
Change is a very hard thing to embrace; even amongst God's most loyal servants. However, if there is going to be a place where leaders can authentically facilitate communities, it needs order.I have seen impoverished churches with a roof and a prayer being held together by the givers of that same community; most of them poor. The church has been the most cherished building we have to date. Even in that regard, it needs a change. The church has become a laughing stock. No one takes our mobility seriously because we have refused innovation. The word of God stands through time unchanged. However, Christ never said that we shouldn't change how it's delivered. This generation is calling for bigger, braver, and better. If we want to be live like Christ, he likened his house to mansions and hospitals, not buildings with coffee products and tables full the latest Christian magazines. There will be no more "playing church". We must train move as an organization. Period. It's going to take the entire body of Christ to get on board.

2020 has met our nation with an unprecedented demand as it pertains to resourcing the wellbeing of people.

The demonic virus, better known as COVID-19 shed a rather interesting light on both our dynamic and our dilemma.

Hospitals have been taken by storm at the enormous need of health care for those who had been taken over by this vicious disease. With almost nowhere to go, even for those who had died from the disease, the hospital had no more room to care for the people. I am sure that in order to get to one hospital in any NYC community; or any other community in our nation, we will dare to pass four or more churches on the way to one hospital. The ratio of closed churches up against functioning hospitals, scream disparity. While churched take up a vast majority in community real-estate, the coronavirus has shown us. We need a change, NOW! **Married2theMission should replace every single church in America**. I know that is a bold statement. **However, it is not about WHO creates the next best idea that gets the credit, rather the audience that reaps its benefit that matters most**. Both past and present has shown us that there is no other way. The church must arise to its much needed conversion in both spirit and in deed. It must rise no longer a prostitute giving 'feel-good' sessions to its community at a high price, but as a warrior bride serving, helping, saving, and loving the world in the name of its groom, Yeshua. (Jesus) We must become a body that protect REAL American Christ-driven values and reestablishes the church as a necessity and not just a religious pillar.

It is with humility and awareness that I ask your help.

New York City, you ready?

Let us get #married2it

"Do not let anyone tell you it cannot be done. No challenge can match the heart and fight and spirit of America. We will not fail. Our country will thrive and prosper again." – Donald Trump

President Trump, You have been charged by God with the leadership of this great nation.

If you are a sincere LEADER, then you know that we are all accountable for the decisions we make therein. The Lord has entrusted you with a power that most could only dream of. You are the ruler in the land of the "free world". Free the people. I have noticed that your time in office has been a very tumultuous one. I can almost attest that besides the nature of such a task, that you also have not had enough WOMEN on your administration. There is also a lack of MINORITY presence. In a country where diversity is its BIGGEST market to the rest of the world, are you willing to consider that you need the help of women? If not, here is a kind reminder that you do. Not only is there a social responsibility on your shoulders, there is a spiritual one as well. If you are familiar with the history of politics by which AMERICA has so faithfully borrowed from Rome, Greece, Babylon, etc. Our country is expected to flourish throughout society alongside its RELIGIOUS power as well. America as it stands is supposed to be nested in the bosom of the Christian faith. If that be **so he advised me to remind you…**

"For to us a child is born, to us a son is given, and the government will be on his shoulders." -ISAIAH 9:6

America..
In a time such as
this... we need
innovative thinkers
who understand
resource and remedy.

..If the president and
the CDC would hear
me Out..

I have a plan.

SHADARIA ALLISON

Married2theMission is a MOVEMENT of Lady Advocates,
united to promote the reconstruction of faith-based organizations by
way of deliberate partnerships with healthcare industry
professionals, and the adjustment of governmental infrastructures in
order to serve real communal needs.

A word from the Author…

America, it is my promise to you that I will go into the nooks and crannies of every undervalued and overlooked city in this nation. I will be the voice for the voiceless. I will talk about the crisis we try to hide. I will make every effort to rally up women and men who will commit to the reform of every urban community in this country. I will continue to challenge American leadership to look at your plight. I will fight for the children and minority population that are at obvious disadvantages in America. **I will continue to encourage churches to be active in their local communities.** I will continue to fight against the injustices displayed towards the "least of these". I will dedicate my talent and abilities to bring awareness and influence to this generation. God loves you. Social injustice has painted a picture of God that resembles hatred. However, I can assure you the very reason he hung on a cross 2020 years ago was for your cause. With every breath I have, I will make that fact as real as the trauma we have endured. He has not forgotten us. **I promise.**

Women, I challenge you in this fight. We were built for more than our image. We were built for great causes, like this one.

Our time is now.

Will you join me?

Let's get #married2it

#MARRIED2IT

www.ingramcontent.com/pod-product-compliance
Lightning Source LLC
Chambersburg PA
CBHW040323010626
45792CB00024B/2106